A NATION OF MANY COLORS

BY JOSHUA NISSENBAUM

Editorial Offices: Glenview, Illinois • Parsippany, New Jersey • New York, New York
Sales Offices: Needham, Massachusetts • Duluth, Georgia • Glenview, Illinois
Coppell, Texas • Ontario, California • Mesa, Arizona

ISBN: 0-328-13515-1

4 5 6 7 8 9 10   V0G1   14 13 12 11 10 09 08 07 06

CONTENTS

Introduction
The Melting Pot

Have you ever heard the phrase "the melting pot" used to describe the United States? No one knows when it was first used. But it first became popular in 1908 when Israel Zangwill wrote a play titled *The Melting Pot.* The play, which attracted a lot of attention, focused on the experiences of early twentieth-century American **immigrants.**

Ever since Zangwill's play, people have used "melting pot" to describe the collection of ethnic groups that have immigrated to the United States. The United States' melting pot grew rapidly in the late 1800s, when millions of immigrants came into the country. Each **newcomer** brought along customs, cultural products, languages, and values, which changed American culture.

The United States' diverse population earned it the nickname "the melting pot."

Many Cubans have reacted to Cuba's government by immigrating to Florida.

Immigrants come to America for all sorts of reasons. Many arrive looking to acquire an education. Others come hoping to find jobs and gain civil rights. Millions journey to the United States to escape from war, starvation, and the cruel government policies they experienced back home.

Immigration to the United States often occurs in waves, as many people of the same ethnic background arrive over the course of several years. For example, from 1959 to 1962, more than 200,000 Cuban immigrants came to Florida. They came because they felt threatened by Fidel Castro's communist form of government. They were also looking forward to obtaining better jobs, civil rights, and educations.

New York City's Chinatown contains block after block of Chinese-run shops and businesses.

Immigrant Communities

Immigrants to the United States are sometimes unprepared for parts of American life. To ease their transition, those that belong to the same ethnic group often settle in the same area, forming a small community. Such communities are spread across the United States. They exist in many major cities, especially the seaports of the East and West Coasts. Immigrant communities are often given names such as "Chinatown," "Koreatown," or "Little Italy," based on the ethnic groups that live in them.

For a newcomer, these communities provide many of the features of home. They also offer a newcomer the chance to adjust to the United States gradually and to keep his or her ethnic identity. Within these communities, immigrants speak their native language, and restaurants, shops, and businesses sell traditional ethnic foods, goods, and services.

Among the most famous immigrant communities are San Francisco's Chinatown, Detroit's Greektown, New York's Little Italy, and the Koreatown in Los Angeles. Each of these immigrant communities has a long and proud tradition. They all feature restaurants and shops that specialize in the foods and products of their residents' homelands. They are also famous for celebrating the holidays of their residents' native cultures.

An immigrant community's restaurants, shops, and other cultural attractions can make it an attractive place to live. This can lead to *gentrification*. Gentrification happens when wealthier people move into a poorer neighborhood. Since wealthier people are willing to pay more for things, they cause the cost of living to go up. The residents of immigrant communities need to work together with local politicians to help solve the problems created by gentrification.

Celebrations of the Chinese New Year include colorful parades.

Immigrants to the United States have to deal with many issues other than gentrification. They need to find places to live. They need to find jobs that can pay for necessities such as food, clothing, and shelter. They have to learn the laws and customs of American society.

Each of these issues creates challenges that immigrants have to overcome in order to be successful. The rest of the book describes the challenges that three separate ethnic groups–Hispanic Americans, African Americans, and Jewish Americans–have faced in the United States. Each of these three groups arrived in the United States under different **circumstances.** Each brought along with them different sets of values and beliefs. But as you will see, the hardships they faced have given them much in common.

The ceremony in which immigrants become citizens marks the end of a long and challenging process.

Many Mexican citizens became Americans as a result of the Mexican-American War.

Chapter One
Hispanic Americans

The first Hispanic Americans came from Mexico. They became Americans in an unusual way. From 1846 to 1848 the United States and Mexico fought the Mexican-American War. The United States won the war in 1848. As a result it took control of land that had belonged to Mexico. This land included parts of what are now the states of California, New Mexico, Nevada, Wyoming, Utah, Colorado, and Arizona.

The Mexicans living on this land were given the choice of staying and becoming Americans, or moving south to Mexico. For various reasons, most Mexicans who found themselves in this situation decided to stay on the American-controlled land. In a sense, these Hispanic Americans didn't "come" to the United States. Rather, the United States came to them!

Spain

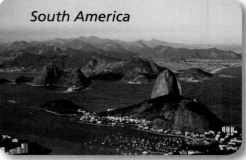
South America

Mexico

A Fast-Growing Ethnic Group

People from Mexico make up more than half of all Hispanics living in the United States. The 2000 Census reports that there were 20,640,711 Mexican Americans living in the United States at the time. The number of Mexican Americans increases each year as more Mexicans immigrate to the United States.

You've now seen the phrase "Hispanic American" used a few times. But do you know what it means? The Census Bureau states that Hispanic Americans are people who have come from Spain and Mexico. Hispanic Americans also come from the Spanish-speaking countries of Central and South America. Hispanic Americans have been one of the country's fastest-growing ethnic groups for several decades. In 2000, an estimated thirty-five million Hispanic Americans lived in the United States.

Of those thirty-five million Hispanic Americans, almost three-quarters lived in Texas, California, New York, and Florida. The population of Hispanic Americans living in California is particularly large. It is estimated that 1.7 million Hispanic Americans live in the city of Los Angeles alone. As high as that number is, it does not include the large number of Hispanic Americans living in the cities surrounding Los Angeles. In comparison, Madrid, Spain, has approximately three million Spanish-speaking residents.

Jennifer Lopez: Star for the Ages

Hispanic Americans are active in politics, the arts, civil rights, and other areas. One of the most well-known Hispanic Americans is Jennifer Lopez, who has enjoyed success as an actress, singer, and businesswoman. Lopez is Puerto Rican by background. Born in 1970, she grew up in New York City's Bronx neighborhood.

Jennifer Lopez has created a business empire from her career as an entertainer.

11

Lopez has starred in several movies and sold millions of recordings. She even has her own perfume! Lopez is currently the highest paid Hispanic American actress. She is also the first woman to have a movie and record album reach number one at the same time.

César Chávez: Fighting for Farmworkers

Before Jennifer Lopez, another famous Hispanic American was César Chávez. Chávez was born in 1927 to a family of migrant farmworkers. His childhood was made difficult by his family's constant moves. When Chávez became a farmworker in the 1950s, he began organizing farmworkers. He **advised** them on ways to gain better pay and improved working conditions. For years, Chávez fought for farmworkers' rights. He died in 1993. The following year, President Bill Clinton awarded Chávez's family the Presidential Medal of Freedom.

César Chávez worked tirelessly to improve conditions for migrant farmworkers.

African Americans were enslaved until 1865. They have struggled to obtain equal rights ever since.

Chapter Two
African Americans

In the history of the United States, African Americans are unique. They are the only immigrant group to come to the United States against their will.

Enslaved Africans were first brought to what would become the United States in 1619. By 1700, the colony of Virginia was importing about 1,000 enslaved Africans each year. The Southern economy depended on enslaved Africans for the labor they provided.

The growth of the cotton and tobacco industries encouraged white Americans to import more and more enslaved Africans. By the start of the Civil War there were about 3.5 million enslaved African Americans. In 1865, slavery was abolished, freeing the enslaved African Americans.

The Civil Rights Movement

Since the abolition of slavery, African Americans have had to battle severe prejudice, or racism, of white Americans. White Americans have had difficulty accepting the fact that African Americans deserve equal rights. In some ways, African Americans are still forced to fight for the equality they deserve.

After World War II, African Americans decided they were no longer going to tolerate racism. Out of their determination grew the civil rights movement. The movement used peaceful methods to promote equality among all Americans. It caused many white Americans to reconsider their views towards African Americans and others. The movement united African Americans as never before, producing leaders such as Martin Luther King, Jr.

The 1960s also saw a renewed interest in African cultural traditions. In 1966, the holiday Kwanzaa was created by an African American political activist named Maulana Ron Karenga. Karenga created Kwanzaa so that African Americans could enjoy elements of traditional African culture. Kwanzaa is celebrated during the last six days of December, ending on New Year's Day. Nearly five million African Americans took part in Kwanzaa in 1990.

After years of struggle, African Americans have created a strong ethnic identity. Music, fashion, sports, and entertainment are all areas that have benefited from African American involvement. In addition, African Americans have made major contributions to science and literature.

The March on Washington, held August 28, 1963, was a highlight of the civil rights movement. Martin Luther King, Jr. gave his famous "I Have a Dream Speech" at this rally.

African Americans in Politics

African Americans account for only 13 percent of the U.S. population. This makes them a minority. Despite this disadvantage in numbers, African Americans have been elected mayors in major cities such as Los Angeles, Philadelphia, Chicago, and New York City. They have also won elections in cities where there are very few African Americans, such as Augusta, Maine, and Denver, Colorado.

African Americans have also gained ground in the federal government. In 1992, Carol Moseley Braun was elected senator of Illinois, making her the first female African American senator. The following year, Ron Brown was named Secretary of Commerce. Before Brown, only Robert Weaver, who was Secretary of Housing and Urban Development during the 1960s, had held such a position.

Willie Brown served as San Francisco's mayor from 1996 to 2004.

Condoleezza Rice has played an important role in giving foreign policy advice to President George W. Bush.

In 2001, President George W. Bush named Colin Powell to serve as Secretary of State and Condoleezza Rice to serve as National Security Advisor. In 2004, Rice replaced Powell as Secretary of State. Both Powell and Rice have given **advice** to President Bush on how to deal with major foreign policy issues. And both are African American.

Many African American politicians of less fame than Powell and Rice are working to improve the lives of African Americans. Groups such as the Congressional Black Caucus (CBC), formed in 1969 to give added strength to African Americans in Congress, have helped reduce inequality over the past few decades by drawing attention to issues affecting African Americans. The CBC and similar organizations will continue to play a major role in guiding African Americans toward a better future.

A monument in Chicago to George Washington, Robert Morris, and Haym Salomon

Chapter Three
Jewish Americans

Jewish people have been in the United States since the 1600s. In Europe, Jews faced anti-Semitism. Anti-Semitism is a form of prejudice that singles out Jewish people. It caused many Jewish people to come to the United States.

From early on, Jewish Americans were eager to assist with the country's development. Haym Salomon, a Polish Jew, helped finance the American Revolution. Such efforts inspired George Washington to send a letter in 1790 to Rhode Island's Jewish American community, promising that they would always be safe in the United States.

Washington's letter was important, given how few Jews lived in the United States at that time. The two thousand Jewish people living in the United States in 1790 made up less than one percent of the country's total population.

Friction Between Different Jewish Groups

In the late 1800s, people from all over Europe immigrated to the United States. Among them were many Jewish people. From 1880 to 1920 approximately two million Jews entered the United States. Many of them were Eastern European Jews escaping the anti-Semitism that flared up in Eastern Europe during the late nineteenth century.

The Jewish Americans who had immigrated in the early 1800s from Germany resented the later Eastern European Jewish immigrants. These earlier Jewish immigrants had worked hard to blend into American society. They feared that the newcomers would upset their position in America and cause anti-Semitism. Most of the Jewish people from Eastern Europe were uneducated and needed assistance in adapting to life in the United States.

Many Russian Jews faced poverty when they first arrived in New York.

In time Jewish Americans would overcome their cultural differences to embrace their common heritage. But in the late 1800s, these differences caused tension. The German Jews considered the Russian Jews to be inferior. The Eastern European Jews felt that the German Jews had given up their Jewish identity.

The majority of Jewish immigrants from Eastern Europe settled in New York City. They lived in a compact community centered in Manhattan's Lower East Side. Life there was very different from what they expected.

Many of the Russian Jewish immigrants had expected life to be easier in America. However, many found themselves living in poverty upon arriving in the United States. They struggled to find work. Many lived in crumbling apartments crammed with dozens of people.

New York's Lower East Side, where many Eastern European Jews lived during the early 1900s.

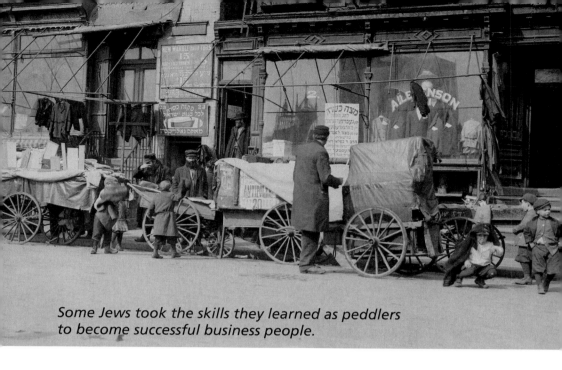
Some Jews took the skills they learned as peddlers to become successful business people.

From Peddlers to Business People

Despite these difficulties, the Eastern European Jews often had a slight advantage over other immigrant groups. Most other European immigrants had been farmers. However, in parts of Europe, Jewish people were not allowed to own land. This forced them to become business people. In Manhattan, which had no farming and focused on business, it helped to have such a background.

As much as the Eastern European Jews were helped by their business experience, they still faced enormous challenges upon arriving in New York. Most of the jobs available to immigrants were already taken. As a result, many Jewish people would buy something small and then sell it on the street for a modest profit. Being a **peddler** like this was tough work. Peddlers often had to **elbow** their way through crowds. They **hustled** their goods to any customers they could attract.

Some Jewish American peddlers were very successful and used their profits to open stores. Jewish immigrants opened famous department stores such as Filene's in Boston. Other Jewish immigrants moved into selling **luxury** goods such as diamonds and fur coats. These early business ventures allowed Jews to move into positions of power and wealth in American society.

During the 1900s much of the Jewish American community moved from the cities to the suburbs. In the process, they blended into mainstream American culture. Jewish Americans were so successful at blending in that in a short time they were seen as being more American than Jewish. Today, many in the Jewish community have called upon American Jews to revive their ethnic heritage.

The United States is a nation of immigrants. Its constant stream of newcomers has given it the most diverse population in history.

Conclusion
Our Diverse Country

Never before has there been a country as diverse as the United States. In the past, cities such as London, Rome, and Hong Kong have attracted diverse populations. But the United States has *many* cities, such as Chicago, New York, and Los Angeles, with lots of different ethnic groups living in them. In New York alone there are more than one hundred different languages spoken!

The ethnic groups that you have read about have done much to contribute to the United States' diversity. At times they have experienced tension both among themselves and with other ethnic groups. But overall they have made our country a far more exciting and interesting place to live!

Glossary

advice *n.* opinion about what should be done; suggestion.

advised *v.* gave advice to.

circumstances *n.* conditions that accompany an act or event.

elbow *v.* to make your way by pushing.

hustled *v.* gotten or sold in a hurried way.

immigrants *n.* people who come into a country or region to live there.

luxury *n.* something pleasant but not necessary.

newcomer *n.* person who has just come or who came not long ago.

peddler *n.* person who travels about selling things carried in a pack or in a truck, wagon, or cart.